A Christmas Quartet:

POETIC REFLECTIONS ON THE NATIVITY

William G. Carter

CSS PUBLISHING COMPANY, INC., LIMA, OHIO

For more information about CSS Publishing Company resources, visit our website at www.csspub.com.

ISBN 0-7880-1844-2
PRINTED IN U.S.A.

To Katherine Ann and Margaret Rose,
who remind me regularly
of the miracle of birth,
the possibility of wonder,
the availability of joy,
and the power of love.

TABLE OF CONTENTS

INTRODUCTION

A number of years ago, I decided to write a Christmas Eve sermon in verse. It seemed like a great idea in early December, but as the days began to hasten on, my decision seemed more and more questionable. About three days before Christmas, I scrapped the idea and put together a traditional sermon on the incarnation.

That sermon was dull. Standing in the pulpit that night, I had the nagging sense that I had somehow betrayed my own sense of wonder and awe. "Surely Christmas Eve deserves something better than this," I mused. Returning home after the last service that night, I pulled the broken couplets from my briefcase and quietly resolved to try again the following year.

It didn't come easily. Part of my struggle came from a decision to avoid being trite, cute, or superficial. There's far too much of those sorts of things at the holidays. If we gather at Christmas to celebrate the birth of Jesus Christ, preachers are under obligation to honor our Lord with theological depth and a clear word of grace. Whoever climbs into the Christian pulpit must be committed to the careful study of scripture, if only to get the message *right*.

Yet the news at Christmas is *so good* that there should also be some delight in our voices. Why *not* a poem, a song, or a dance? The nativity stories of Matthew and Luke have inspired an enormous quantity of art and music over the centuries. By creating something fresh and new for Christmas, we participate in the creativity of God. We give room for the Word to touch our flesh. Those convictions nipped at my heels for many months, until I resigned myself to sit in an overstuffed chair and finish the project.

It took me a whole year to glue together that first sermonic poem, which is printed here under the title, "For The Shepherds." As I read the words to a hushed Christmas Eve congregation, I feared the poem was going right over the heads of the Friendly Beasts and a few of their parents. I was wrong: everybody was simply paying attention. The rhythm of the words kept the concentration of extra-charged children. The novelty of the event helped weary adults to tune in as never before. When the service concluded, one worshiper after another asked the question that made me tremble: "Are you going to write another poem for next year?"

Over the next few years I wrote three more poems, honoring Mary, Joseph, and the Wise Men. All were originally presented as Christmas Eve sermons at First Presbyterian Church, Clarks Summit, Pennsylvania. I am fortunate to serve a congregation that encourages my creativity. Many friends, both inside and outside of the congregation, have kept suggesting that these poems be published for the benefit of a wider audience. Weary after years of resisting, I have given in.

I have no illusion that this is good poetry; if anything, it will quickly end up on the ash heap of holiday doggerel. Yet I've done my best to receive the good news of Christmas and speak it in a way that people can hear. If the Word gets through to anybody, to God be the glory!

To make these rhyming sermons helpful to others, each is preceded by a brief chapter that offers some historical and theological understanding of the characters of the poem. I have studied the best available scholarship on Mary, Joseph, the shepherds, and the Wise Men, and tried to share something of what I have discovered. While there is little in these prose chapters that is radical or new, they do attempt to "set up" each of the poems. Busy preachers, for instance, may find this material helpful as they prepare for sermons and Bible studies.

At the back of the book, there are suggested outlines for three different Christmas Eve services and a service on the day of Epiphany. These services are built on a "lessons and carols" format, where each scripture reading is interpreted by a familiar carol. The brief liturgies can easily be adapted for Advent gatherings, Bible studies, and potluck dinners. The scripture texts and songs have been carefully chosen, so that the message of the sermons will be properly emphasized.

One last thing: these poetic sermons are intended to be spoken, not read. There is a rhythm written into each poem. I encourage you to read them aloud and listen for the implicit syncopation.

This may take a bit of practice, since the rhymes are occasionally imprecise. Some syllables will dance easily, while others will need your encouragement.

It is my heartfelt hope that this little book will bring alive for you the good news of Christ's birth. After you read it, I hope you will try your own hand at bringing the Gospel alive for others.

May the wonder and joy of Christ fill your heart, mind, and soul.

William G. Carter
Christmas 2000

BELIEVING A BEAM OF LIGHT:
MARY'S FAITH AND OURS
Luke 1:26-38

> 26 In the sixth month the angel Gabriel was sent by
> God to a town in Galilee called Nazareth, 27 to a vir-
> gin engaged to a man whose name was Joseph, of the
> house of David. The virgin's name was Mary. 28 And
> he came to her and said, "Greetings, favored one! The
> Lord is with you." 29 But she was much perplexed by
> his words and pondered what sort of greeting this might
> be. 30 The angel said to her, "Do not be afraid, Mary,
> for you have found favor with God. 31 And now, you
> will conceive in your womb and bear a son, and you
> will name him Jesus. 32 He will be great, and will be
> called the Son of the Most High, and the Lord God will
> give to him the throne of his ancestor David. 33 He
> will reign over the house of Jacob forever, and of his
> kingdom there will be no end." 34 Mary said to the
> angel, "How can this be, since I am a virgin?" 35 The
> angel said to her, "The Holy Spirit will come upon you,
> and the power of the Most High will overshadow you;
> therefore the child to be born will be holy; he will be
> called Son of God. 36 And now, your relative Eliza-
> beth in her old age has also conceived a son; and this
> is the sixth month for her who was said to be barren.
> 37 For nothing will be impossible with God." 38 Then
> Mary said, "Here am I, the servant of the Lord; let it
> be with me according to your word." Then the angel
> departed from her.

A young girl sits on the edge of the bed. Her room is simply
furnished. We see a small oil lamp and a water jug, a couple of
blankets and a wrinkled rug. She draws our gaze as she sits near
the center of the picture, yet we immediately notice her attention
is directed elsewhere. She cocks her head at a curious angle as she
looks toward a luminous beam of light at the foot of her bed.

This is how Henry Ossawa Tanner painted the Gabriel's visit to Mary. Visitors to the Philadelphia Museum of Art will stop in their tracks to ponder the same mystery that captures that young girl. We see in this painting the vulnerable humanity of a peasant girl, in stark contrast to the awesome otherness of a heavenly being. That is precisely Mary's situation in the first chapter of Luke.

Suspend, if you can, the fact that Mary is second only to Jesus in receiving adoration from Christians. She is a young girl from a small town. An angel appears out of the blue, without any reference to her virtues. For reasons known only to God, Mary is chosen to bear the Christ child.

For centuries, pious Christians have attempted to explain God's decision. Why Mary? In 1854, the Roman Catholic Church decreed Mary was free from sin. After all, it was reasoned, she was the mother of Jesus, who came to redeem us from sin. A Redeemer from sin must be without sin. Therefore, in order for Jesus to be sinless, his mother must also be sinless.

So the church wrote:

> We declare, pronounce and define: the doctrine that maintains that the most Blessed Virgin Mary in the first instant of her conception, by a unique grace and privilege of the omnipotent God and in consideration of the merits of Christ Jesus the Savior of the human race, was preserved free from all stain of original sin, is a doctrine revealed by God and therefore must be firmly and constantly held by all the faithful.[1]

Why Mary? In medieval times, Anselm of Canterbury composed a treatise titled, "Why God Became Man." He claimed Mary's selection had to do with her gender. God chose Mary, not because she was sinless, but because she was a daughter of Eve, our primal mother who should be blamed for human sin. In Anselm's words:

> It is most fitting for the medicine of sin and the cause of our salvation to be born of a woman, just as the sin of man and the condemnation took its beginning from a woman. Also, lest women despair of sharing in the

12

*lot of the blessed, since such great evil came from a
woman, it is right that such great good should come
from a woman, to renew their hope. And paint this too:
if the cause of all evil for the human race was a virgin,
it is still more fitting for the cause of all good to be a
virgin.*[2]

Why Mary? In a small fishing village in Nicaragua, some peasants were talking about this story before mass. One of them said:

*God wanted his son to be born in a pigsty, in a stable.
He wanted his son to belong to the poor class, right?
If God wanted him to be born to a rich lady, that lady
would have had a room reserved ... especially arriving in her condition.*[3]

Why did God choose her? Was she free from sin? The Bible
makes no such claim. Was she a Second Eve who could undo the
work of the first Eve? That wrongly assumes all the blame for
human sin should be pinned on Eve, and conveniently overlooks
that Adam took a bite out of the same forbidden fruit without rais-
ing any questions. Did God choose Mary because she was poor, a
peasant among peasants? Certainly she was poor,[4] but there is no
obvious privilege in poverty.

The reason behind Mary's selection is a mystery known only
to God. As she enters the drama from stage right, the spotlight is
on God, not Mary. God sends the angel Gabriel to announce the
birth. The announcement is made in the sixth month of Elizabeth's
pregnancy, tying it to God's prior announcement of another un-
common birth. Gabriel sings praises of the child:

*"He will be great,
He will be called Son of the Most High God,
God will give him the throne of David,
and he will reign forever."*   — Luke 1:32-33

No sooner does the angel catch a breath after singing his hal-
lelujah when Mary asks, "How can this be?" It is the second time

that question is asked in the Gospel of Luke. Just one chapter earlier, the priest Zechariah asked that question when he heard he would become the father of John. In that instance, the angel struck him speechless. It was appropriate punishment for a religious leader who doubted the power of God; obviously Zechariah had nothing to say.

For the time being, Mary gets off far easier. Why shouldn't a young girl question such astonishing news? Even at her innocent age, she probably knew enough about the birds and the bees to wonder how this birth could happen. The pregnancy would always be regarded as a scandal in her small town. There was no way to anticipate how her beloved Joseph would respond to the news. What's more, angels come and go, but children remain. Any beatific birth announcement would be tempered by the hard realities of late night feedings, colic, and potty training.

As Luke tells her story, he suggests Mary was a reflective soul who looked for the deeper implications of the events in her life. Three times he says she "pondered" or "treasured" the words of others: the announcement of the angel (1:29), the announcement of the shepherds (2:19), and her son's announcement that he must be in his Father's house (2:51). While we can only guess at the content of her thoughts, Luke's verbs imply Mary did a lot of deliberate thinking about the Child and his larger role in the world.

This has led some to regard her as the "first theologian" of the church. As Patrick Miller notes:

> We can be confident that thinking about the meaning of this child, about what God was doing in him, and about the mystery of how people (poor people, academics, and just plain "church" folk) responded to him in wonder and praise, whether encountering him as a tiny helpless baby or as a precocious adolescent was something that must have gone on all the time in Mary's mind. She was not one of the rabbis, not one of the persons called or appointed to the study of God's ways as found in Scripture and the story of Israel. We have no book of Scripture written by this woman. She was simply the mother of this child. But the first musings

*over his significance, the first christological reflection,
began with the woman who brought him forth in pain
and nursed him on her breast. While we do not know
all she thought, we know that her theological reflection never ceased, for such is the way of mothers with
their children.*[5]

One year, some of our church members dramatized the poem
that follows this chapter.[6] In the midst of the presentation, the choir
sang a beautiful anthem titled "Mary, Did You Know?"[7] Following the service, a young mother emerged from the sanctuary in
tears. "For the very first time," she sniffed, "I realized that God
has a purpose for my kids, too, and someday it might bring me
some heartbreak, just like Mary. I guess every mother has to wrestle
with these things." Maybe so.

In her brilliant book, *Mary: Glimpses of the Mother of Jesus*,
Beverly Gaventa notes the difference between the shepherd's awe-
struck arrival and Mary's "pondering." She writes, "The verbs that
describe Mary's response constitute neither wonder nor praise but
perhaps secrecy or even isolation."[8] Who knows what deep thoughts
swirl in a mother's heart?

Since the Gospel writers are primarily interested in Mary's
Son, they maintain a respectful distance from his mother. At times,
her role is downplayed. In John's Gospel, for instance, the mother
of Jesus is never named. She is merely "the mother of Jesus."[9]

Matthew and Mark name her in a handful of stories, but they
grant her no special privileges for her family ties. According to
Mark, Jesus' family attempted to restrain him one day after he was
accused by his opponents of being crazy. At one point he shrugs
them off, saying, "Who are my mother and brothers?" Looking at
those around him, he proclaims, "Here are my mother and my
brothers! Whoever does the will of God is my brother and sister
and mother" (Mark 3:19b-35).

It is instructive, however, that Luke sees Mary as a crucial
member of the first Christian community. She is the first person in
Luke to profess belief in God. With prophetic vigor, she is the first
Christian preacher, proclaiming God's activity in the Magnificat

15

(Luke 1:46-55). And she is named among the circle of the believers who gathered in the upper room after the death, resurrection, and ascension of Jesus. As Luke tells us in his second volume, the Acts of the Apostles: "All these were constantly devoting themselves to prayer, together with certain women, including Mary the mother of Jesus, as well as his brothers" (Acts 1:14).

Mary plays a key role in the opening section of Luke's Gospel. So much so, in fact, that I have come to think she might have been a primary source for the writer of the third Gospel.[10] I realize this may be a romantic notion (imagine a scribe asking, "So, Mary, when did you first think there was something special about your son?"). Yet there is simply so much information about the birth and childhood of Jesus that is reported only in Luke: the birth of Zechariah's son, the annunciation, the greeting of Elizabeth, the appearance of the shepherds, the blessing and warning of Simeon, the disappearance of Jesus when he was twelve years old. Where else could Luke have heard these stories — except from the mother of Jesus?

Regardless of her role in telling the story of Jesus, historical or otherwise, it is clear that Mary is held up as a role model for all believers. That is why we honor her at Christmas. In the Gospel of Luke, there's a brief scene where a woman in a crowd is overwhelmed with joy at the words and deeds of Jesus. As Jesus passes by, she cries out, "Blessed is the womb that bore you and the breasts that nursed you!"

Jesus replies, "Blessed rather are those who hear the word of God and obey it!" (Luke 11:27-28).

I think he was talking about his mother. For how does the story of our redemption begin? Mary says, "Let it be with me according to your word" (Luke 1:38).

---

1. From the papal bull *Ineffibilis Deus*, 1854; reprinted in Hugh T. Kerr, editor, *Readings in Christian Thought* (Nashville: Abingdon Press, 1966), p. 245.

2. Anselm of Canterbury, "Why God Became Man," *A Scholastic Miscellany*, p. 154.

3. Ernesto Cardenal, *The Gospel in Solentiname, volume I* (Maryknoll, New York: Orbis Books), p. 48.

4. According to Luke 2:22-24, Mary and Joseph offered a ritual sacrifice of "a pair of turtledoves or two young pigeons." That was the alternative for a woman too poor to afford a sheep, as allowed by Leviticus 12:8.

5. Patrick D. Miller, "The church's first theologian," *Theology Today,* October 1999, pp. 293-296.

6. My friend Bob London has adapted the poem, "Mary, Ponder This" to serve as the centerpiece of an intergenerational Christmas pageant. Unfortunately the script could not be printed in this volume. Bob is a lifelong Christian Educator who pays careful detail to the words and symbols of that poem. I am grateful for his generous help with this project, and should note that Bob is already immortalized in the poem, "For the Shepherds," as one of the three volunteers who came to Christmas Eve in bathrobes and took part in that year's pageant. Bob's script is available from First Presbyterian Church, 300 School Street, Clarks Summit, Pennsylvania 18411. Contact the church office for details.

7. "Mary, Did You Know?" by Mark Lowry and Buddy Green, arranged by Fred Bock, and published by Fred Bock Music Company (BG2326).

8. Beverly Roberts Gaventa, *Mary: Glimpses of the Mother of Jesus* (Minneapolis: Fortress Press, 1999), p. 61.

9. See John 2:1-5, 2:12, 6:42, and 19:25-27.

10. Luke begins his book by letting us know he has done his homework: "Since many have undertaken to set down an orderly account of the events that have been fulfilled among us, just as they were handed on to us by those who from the beginning were eyewitnesses and servants of the word, I too decided, after investigating everything carefully from the very first, to write an orderly account for you, most excellent Theophilus, so that you may know the truth concerning the things about which you have been instructed" (1:1-4).

MARY, PONDER THIS

"Mary treasured all these words and pondered them in her heart."
(Luke 2:19)

Christmas is hustle and bustle and noise.
There are stockings to fill and piles of toys.
We have trees to put up, decorate, and maintain.
There are meals to make, folks to entertain.
Tonight, as a break, let me make a suggestion:
that we pause for a moment of quiet reflection
To think about Christmas, which we hold so dear,
and to focus on Mary, who held these words near.
The scriptures have told us that Mary did treasure
the tidings from shepherds that came beyond measure:
"The Babe in the manger is born to be king
creation rejoices, and angels do sing.
  Mary, ponder this ..."

The Annunciation (*Luke 1:26-38*)
It began with an angel who came unannounced.
For no reason we know, for no virtues that count,
the angel appeared and foretold a new birth.
Mary was shocked, and fell to the earth.
"Fear not," said the angel (and I pause to remind us
that angels strike fear whenever they find us!).
This angel found Mary and then he declared,
"God will make you pregnant, so don't you be scared.
The Spirit of God, who dispels all the gloom,
will implant the world's Savior inside of your womb.
So blessed are you, and full of God's grace!
Our King's countenance will resemble your face."
She said, "Let it be, as you say in your word,
for I am a maiden who will serve the Lord."
Then Gabriel vanished right out of her sight,
and Mary did ponder these things in the night.
  Mary, ponder this.

Now, angels have half-lives.[1] Their whispers diminish
as time passes quickly and other things finish.
What once was so clear can fade from our view.
So faith, then, is needed to hold what is true.
Faith — that's the ticket! We need to believe
that God will do more than we can conceive.
The only faith that I think is worth having
is faith that will think and seek understanding.
For Luke, Mary is the first true believer.
She said, "Yes," to an angel and became a conceiver.
Yet here is an idea worth putting in motion:
young mother Mary was our first theologian.
She *thought* about what in the world God was doing.
not content to take Mystery without also knowing
that God has some reasons beneath each occurrence
and God is now working. I give my assurance.

    Mary, ponder this.

Visit with Elizabeth (*1:39-56*)
She went to the highlands in her first trimester
and stayed with Elizabeth, a kind of sequester.
The sign to confirm what the angel made known
was a curious pregnancy in a cousin of her own.
Elizabeth was an unusual mother.
Too old to be pregnant, yet one way or other,
the Spirit gave life to her and her man.
And in the grand scheme, it was part of God's plan.
Although they lived long, in the twilight of years,
and barrenness embarrassed them and brought only tears,
God gave them a boy who arrived in a flash.
The son was called John and he loved a good splash.
He took on the cloak of the prophets of old
and preached a hard Word in words that were bold.
John stood at the end of a long prophets' line,
the death of the old, in the changing of time.
For even as he lay in his mother's womb,
he pointed ahead to the empty tomb.

John kicked, and he leaped, and he danced with great mirth,
and all of this happened before Jesus' birth.
When Jesus arrived, it became new creation,
and Israel's light was shined bright for each nation.
In Mary's new Child, the ages would turn,
and we would meet God, for whom our hearts yearn.
The low would be lifted, the lofty brought down,
and God would be glorified within every town.
 Mary pondered this.

Birth and Adoration (*Luke 2:1-20*)
The months passed by quickly, and Mary increased
in wisdom and width and deep inner peace.
Somehow she knew that God would be near.
It gave a foundation and dispelled her fear.
At the end of her term, through Caesar's decree,
she went on a trip with Joseph to see
the city of Bethlehem, where Joseph had roots.
Caesar required this, with soldiers' boots.
And while they were there, the time came for birth.
All heaven was waiting for God to touch earth.
Not protected from pain, not protected from joy,
young Mary gave birth to her first little boy.
Then herders arrived in the middle of night,
reeking of angels, dazzled by light.
They spoke what they heard from a message quite wild,
that God had come down and was here, in this Child.
Joseph just stood there, unsure of his place,
while Mary remembered with tears on her face.
For Gabriel said so. She recalled his part.
The shepherds confirmed what she knew in her heart.
 Mary pondered this.

Twice in the Temple (*Luke 2:22-35; 2:41-51*)
They went to the temple to dedicate her son,
and Simeon appeared and said, "He's the One!"
We've been waiting for him. He comes to console us."

The cry startled all who heard the great fuss.
Mary was shaken and clutched her young lad.
She withdrew in fear, not the least bit glad.
Simeon spooked her, I tell you no lie.
He said, "I've seen Christ. At last I can die."
If that didn't frighten her, listen to this!
The old man turned toward her and said with a hiss:
"A sword will pierce you, O young mother Mary."
The words from that man made her feel wary.
She should have known then that her life would know grief,
that sorrow and joy would be mixed with belief.

But then twelve years later, at Passover time,
they went back to temple, the steps they did climb.
They sat through a seder and retold the story
how God set them free in a great show of glory.
The festival ended. The family went home.
The crowd was so large that no one did know
that Jesus stayed back to discuss with teachers
how God is inclined toward all of his creatures.
When she finally found him, his mother was furious.
The teachers were awestruck. Jesus was curious.
He spoke of his Father and she realized then
that one day, years later, she'd lose him again.
And this pierced her heart with great pain unmatched.
For long before birth, they had been attached.
They were part of each other. He grew in her womb.
But one day he'd leave her to face a dark tomb.
He stared down Old Death and defeated the grave.
He died, but he lives. And he still comes to save!
As far as she cared, he was always her son.
Yet he belongs to the world, for great deeds he has done.
    Mary, ponder this.

Conclusion
This story is Mary's. She locked it away
until someone wanted to know what to say

about this man Jesus, who gave up his life
to conquer the demons and enter our strife.
I think it was Luke whom her stories did tell.
He retold her tales in his good Godspell.
Where else would we know all about Jesus' birth,
if not from his mother who lived here on earth?
A birth among peasants would hardly inspire,
at least until after the Pentecost fire.
So friends, hear the news, and conceive of this:
that God comes down toward us and offers a kiss.
Hold this as treasure and think in your heart.
Trust this announcement and so play your part.
     Friends, ponder this.

With each new experience we're busy, for sure.
It's only our pondering which makes things endure.
We can't simply take each event on the surface,
especially if God is at work in God's purpose.
This life has deep meaning for those who reflect.
More happens each day than we can detect.
If Mary can treasure and ponder her son,
then we must do likewise. For he is the One
whom we come to honor and worship this night.
Born among shadows, he comes to shine light.
Born among peasants, Jesus comes to honor
the meek of the earth and broken-down sinner.
Born to pierce proud hearts and lift up the low.
Born as our Lord to do more than we know.
So we need to ponder the place we will give
to the Child of God who comes here to live
among us, within us, beyond us. Believe!
God gives birth to more than we can conceive.
     Friends, ponder this.

---

1. This is Bill Leety's insight, suggested by his poem, "Half-Life of an Angel."
   The idea is drawn from nuclear energy, where an explosion has diminishing
   effect as time passes.

IN PRAISE OF JOSEPH
Matthew 1:18-25

18 Now the birth of Jesus the Messiah took place in this way. When his mother Mary had been engaged to Joseph, but before they lived together, she was found to be with child from the Holy Spirit. 19 Her husband Joseph, being a righteous man and unwilling to expose her to public disgrace, planned to dismiss her quietly. 20 But just when he had resolved to do this, an angel of the Lord appeared to him in a dream and said, "Joseph, son of David, do not be afraid to take Mary as your wife, for the child conceived in her is from the Holy Spirit. 21 She will bear a son, and you are to name him Jesus, for he will save his people from their sins." 22 All this took place to fulfill what had been spoken by the Lord through the prophet: 23 "Look, the virgin shall conceive and bear a son, and they shall name him Emmanuel," which means, "God is with us." 24 When Joseph awoke from sleep, he did as the angel of the Lord commanded him; he took her as his wife, 25 but had no marital relations with her until she had borne a son; and he named him Jesus.

Of all the characters in the manger scene, Joseph is the one who stands furthest in the shadows. Mary hovers over the child. Shepherds bluster their way in the door, reeking of angels. The Wise Men, once they finally arrive, draw near in reverence and generosity. But Joseph remains at the edge of the Christmas picture.

We name churches after him and call him a saint. But the fact is, we don't know much about Joseph.

Matthew begins his Gospel by relaying information about Joseph's family tree: "The father of Joseph was Jacob, whose father was Matthan, whose father was Eleazar, whose father was Eliud" ... all the way back to King David (Matthew 1:15-16). The writer makes the point that Joseph came from the house and lineage of David, who was the greatest king in Israel's memory.

Luke says that too, although Luke does not agree on the details. Luke says: "Joseph was the son of Heli, son of Matthat, son of Melchi, son of Jannai" ... all the way back to David (Luke 3:23-24). We know where Joseph came from, although we are not sure about the details.

We don't know for certain *where* Joseph lived, either. If you read the Gospel of Matthew, you might conclude that Joseph and Mary lived in a house in Bethlehem (2:11). When King Herod became angry over the birth of Jesus, the family fled to Egypt. After Herod's death, they traveled to the northern town of Nazareth (2:23), and that is where Jesus grew up.

The Gospel of Luke says, "No, that's not quite right." According to Luke, Joseph lived in the country of Nazareth when Mary became pregnant. The emperor Augustus decreed a census. Joseph and Mary went to Bethlehem from Nazareth, the town where they were living, because Bethlehem was the ancestral town of King David and his descendants.

Meanwhile the Gospel of Mark says nothing about Joseph at all. In the thirteenth chapter of Matthew, the writer alludes in passing that Joseph was a carpenter (13:55). In a parallel verse, however, Mark doesn't mention Joseph at all. Instead he says *Jesus* was the carpenter (Mark 6:3).

That is virtually all we know about Joseph from the scriptures. He had traces of royal blood in his veins, which had been diluted over the centuries. His royal lineage may not have counted for much in a time of Roman military occupation, but it *was* royal blood. Joseph was also a carpenter who worked with wood. That is all we know, apart from Matthew 1:18-25. Then we learn something else: *Joseph was a righteous man.* He lived according to the justice of God. For that detail alone, we praise him.

Our problem is trying to understand his righteousness. That term "righteousness" is a word that occurs frequently in Matthew's book. While righteousness is the Old Testament virtue of those who keep the Law of God, that is not necessarily the meaning of the word in this text.

Why is Joseph called "righteous"? In his commentary on the Christmas stories, Raymond Brown notes that three explanations have been offered through the centuries.[1]

The first is that Joseph is righteous because *he is kind and merciful*. In the words of Psalm 112, "Happy are those who fear the Lord, who greatly delight in his commandments ... They rise in the darkness as a light for the upright; they are gracious, merciful, and righteous" (112:1, 4). The qualities of graciousness and mercy are identified with the virtue of being right with God. According to this view, Joseph's goodness is the reason why he was unwilling to expose Mary's scandalous pregnancy in a public way. Undoubtedly this is true, but it doesn't explain why Joseph needed to be told by the angel to take Mary into his home. Joseph was sufficiently gracious and merciful to resolve to dismiss Mary quietly, but not merciful and gracious enough to take her immediately as his wife. God needed to intervene before he made that decision.

The second explanation for the righteousness of Joseph has to do with *his piety*. Some Christians through the centuries have held the view that when Joseph heard Mary was pregnant, he immediately believed the child came by the Holy Spirit. According to this perspective, Joseph was awe-struck that God might choose his betrothed Mary to bear the Savior. Yet he worried he might be unsuitable, saying to himself, "How dare I take God's chosen vessel as my spouse?" Out of reverence for God and deep respect for Mary, Joseph decided to break off his engagement. His reverence and respect, therefore, is why some people thought he was righteous.

As pious as it sounds, this view assumes more than is reasonable. There is no reason from the story to assume that Joseph was holier than anybody else. He is faced with a difficult dilemma, and chooses to take the high road by avoiding the potential scandal. What's more, there is no evidence that he learned about the cause of the pregnancy right away. The reader of Matthew's story learns Mary has become pregnant through the Holy Spirit before Joseph does. Joseph does not discover the Holy Spirit's work until it is revealed to him in a dream — and the dream takes place *after* he has decided to send Mary away.

The third notion of righteousness pertains to *obedience to the Law*. The righteous person takes the Law seriously, knowing God gave it to us and expects us to keep every piece of it.

Just imagine how Joseph felt when the news came that Mary was expecting. He knew he was not the father of the child. No matter how much he loved her, he must have stayed up all night thinking about it, the commandments of God staring him in the face. The Law was clear: "If a young woman becomes married, and there is proof that she has been with another man, the people shall drag her out of her father's house and stone her to death. You shall purge the evil from your midst" (Deuteronomy 22:20-21).

Joseph was a righteous man. He knew that commandment. But he displayed mercy for Mary and awe for what God had done in her womb. Even though he was initially afraid to take Mary as his wife, he went beyond what the Law required.

It seems to me that the writer of Matthew is teaching us another, broader view of righteousness. His intent becomes clearer when we read the story of Joseph's dream in the larger context of the first Gospel.

By beginning his book with a genealogy, Matthew suggests that Joseph could find a way forward by recalling God's unusual actions in history. At first glance, the genealogy tells of an orderly progression of generations. There is a righteous order to human history, three sets of fourteen (a perfect seven, times two) generations. From the call of Father Abraham to the dynasty of King David to the exile into Babylon to the birth of the Christ, God has acted in the history of the Jewish people in decisive and orderly ways.

Well, at first it seems like an orderly progression. The further we dig in, the quicker we discover some odd surprises. For one thing, Matthew is summarizing the genealogy rather than detailing every specific father and son connection. Historians tells us that Matthew has left a few generations out. For another thing, the writer intentionally includes a number of *women* in this proper Jewish genealogy. And not just any women! He recalls Tamar (1:3), Rahab (1:5), Ruth (1:5), the "wife of Uriah" (1:6) ... and Mary (1:16). All of them are recipients of strange grace and actresses in

God's unusual drama of redemption. Since God is at work, Joseph has every reason to expect the birth of Jesus will be filled with surprising details.

Do you see what Matthew is doing? He prepares us for the story of Joseph by signaling that (a) God will continue his redemptive history through the birth of Jesus, and (b) God will be acting in some astonishing way. The writer can announce, "The birth of Jesus the Messiah took place in this way." It happened through the power of God, who moves toward each of us in perfect righteousness. God's righteousness is revealed as God acts toward us with uncalculated love and generosity, rather than sticking to the strict letter of the Law.

"Joseph, don't be afraid," says the angel. Let this son be born into your family, that the child of God might be the Son of David.

"Joseph, fear not!" This birth is not Mary's fault. We have a God who is capable of acting in surprising ways. Just remember Tamar, Bathsheba, Ruth ...

"Don't be afraid, Joseph. When the child is born, you shall name him 'Yeshua,' or *Savior*, for he shall save his people from the sins they commit and the messes they create."

Joseph's first waking act is to obey the Lord's command, as given through the angel. It will require a *costly obedience* to God. We don't need too much imagination to think of the costs Joseph faced: the personal embarrassment, the murmurs among townspeople, the limitations of becoming a husband and a father all at once, the preposterous winks shared with Mary, to say nothing of receiving a gift for which he did not ask. For Matthew, Joseph is the first Christian disciple. In the first two chapters of this book, the quality of Joseph's discipleship is measured by his willingness to do whatever the living God tells him.

From the very beginning of the Gospel of Matthew, we are taught a new definition of righteousness. Joseph could have stuck to the letter of the Law and abandoned Mary. By choosing to leave her quietly, he intended to keep the Law without pushing it to its extreme punishments. Yet an angel of the Lord tells him to listen to a commandment from God which comes from beyond the established law. God calls Joseph to overlook the literal commandments

27

so that the commandments can be fulfilled in far deeper ways. There is a living script given for Joseph to follow which cannot be reduced to a fixed word on paper. Joseph, like the rest of us, is called to pursue a higher righteousness which far exceeds the lifeless obedience of the scribes and Pharisees. It's the kind of righteousness which comes to us *through* the words of scripture, but ultimately must be lived out *off the page.*

In his commentary on the Gospel of Matthew, Tom Long writes:

> *Joseph becomes, therefore, a model for the Christian life. He learns that being truly righteous does not mean looking up a rule in a book and then doing the "right thing"; it means wrestling with the complexities of a problem, listening for the voice of God, and then doing God's thing. To be a faithful disciple means prayerfully seeking to discover what God is doing in the difficult situations we face. How is God at work here to show mercy and saving power? Being righteous is never simply being pure and good in the abstract; genuine righteousness is always joining with God to do God's work in the world.*[2]

The lesson Joseph learns is the same lesson that Jesus taught to his disciples. As Mary's child grew up to say, "Unless your righteousness exceeds that of the scribes and Pharisees, you will never enter the kingdom of heaven. You have heard that it was said to those of ancient times, 'You shall not murder'; but I say unto you, Don't insult a brother or sister" (Matthew 5:21-22).

"You have heard that it was said, 'Limit your retaliation to an eye for an eye and a tooth for a tooth.' But I say to you, Do not resist an evildoer. But if anyone strikes you on the right cheek, take the initiative by turning the other also" (5:38-42).

"You have heard that it was said, 'You shall love your neighbor and hate your enemy.' But I say to you, Love your enemies and pray for those who persecute you, so that you may be children of your Father in heaven. You see, God is generous to the evil and the good, without distinction" (5:43-44).

Go the extra mile. Make the deeper commitment. Forgive the sinner seven times seventy. Listen for God to speak *through* the written rules, and then *go further*. Go beyond what you first thought God required. You can do it, because our hero Joseph did so before us.

In the thirteenth century, an anonymous poet wrote a dialogue that interprets Joseph's dilemma in taking Mary as his wife. It is a conversation between Joseph and the angel that takes place in a dream. The angel begins:

> *Marvel not, Joseph, on Mary mild;*
> *Forsake her not, though she be with child.*

Joseph replies:

> *I, Joseph, wonder how this may be,*
> *That Mary waxed great when I and she*
> *Ever have lived in chastity;*
> *If she be with child, it is not by me.*

So the angel explains:

> *Marvel not, Joseph.*
> *Marvel not, Joseph.*
> *The Holy Ghost with merciful distance*
> *In here hath entered without offense,*
> *God and man conceived by his presence,*
> *And she virgin pure without violence.*
> *Marvel not, Joseph.*
> *Marvel not, Joseph.*

Joseph ponders these things in his heart, and says:

> *What the angel of God to me doth say*
> *I, Joseph, must and will humbly obey,*
> *Or else privately I would have stolen away,*
> *But now I will serve here 'til that day.*

29

With that, the angel makes its final proclamation:

> *Marvel not, Joseph.*
> *Marvel not, Joseph.*
> *Joseph, thou shalt here maid and mother find,*
> *Here the Son, redeemer of all humankind*
> *Thy forebears of pains to unbind;*
> *Therefore muse not this matter in thy mind.*
> *Marvel not, Joseph.*
> *Marvel not, Joseph.*[3]

When he awoke, Joseph, the Son of David, did what he was told. He took Mary into his home; and his righteousness prepared the way for the salvation of the world.

----

1. Raymond E. Brown, *The Birth of the Messiah* (New York: Doubleday, 1977), pp. 126-127.

2. Thomas G. Long, *Matthew* (Louisville: Westminster John Knox, 1996), p. 15.

3. *An Advent Sourcebook*, ed. Thomas J. O. Gorman (Chicago: Liturgy Training Publications, 1988), p. 107.

JOSEPH, JUST STAND THERE
Matthew 1:18-25

There once was a boy, about six years of age,
who played his first role on the dramatic stage.
The scene, set in church, was an annual show:
a pageant for Christmas, when fresh was the snow.
He put on a bathrobe, a towel on his head.
And he portrayed Joseph, a figure now dead.
He dressed like the carpenter from Nazareth,
while Mary was played by a young girl named Beth.

He went to the church on a Saturday morning
to practice the pageant so he needed no warning
to know what to do, where to stand, what to say.
(Because, as you know, it's a really big play!)
The director, Miss Jones, taught a Sunday school class
and handled her mob with firm hands and panache.
Each costume was made by the first day of Advent,
as Miss Jones oversaw each small piece of the pageant.
She painted some palm trees on cardboard as art,
and carried a clipboard that listed each part.
The children came dressed and stood in their places
as their dear director put them through the paces.
The boy who played Joseph stood tall at the start,
for he knew his role was an important part.
Well, that was the thought which he had in his head
until Miss Jones spoke up and said something instead:
"All we need you to do is to walk down the aisle,
turn around at the end, and just stand there and smile."
"Wait!" he replied. "Have I nothing to say?
Have I nothing to do? Have I no part to play?"
"No," said Miss Jones, "you have nothing to do.
Joseph, just stand by the girl dressed in blue.
    Joseph, just stand there."

Now that is a scene that I sometimes remember
whenever we come to the midst of December.
Reflecting on Joseph, let's say it is true
that, yes, he just stood there, with nothing to do.
The story we heard does reveal that, maybe,
old Joe had no part in producing the Baby.
He had nothing to do. No passion to show.
The kid wasn't his; and his wife told him so.
Not easy to hear, or so goes the story.
When he heard the news, Joseph welled up with worry.
He thought he'd divorce her, and then keep it quiet.
A Baby from heaven? Oh, come on, who will buy it?
Yet then came a dream some time late in the night.
An angel appeared, filling Joseph with fright.
"Fear not," said the angel. "Take Mary as wife.
The Child in her womb will soon come to bring life
to all those in darkness. To find those now lost.
It will not come cheap, but at significant cost.
I tell you, this Child is Emmanuel.
In him shall the fullness of God choose to dwell.
So, Joseph, just stand there. Take Mary as wife,
and God will send Jesus to end all the strife."
        Joseph just stood there.

"A just man," says Matthew, and I trust his word.
'Cause if I were old Joseph, I'd think it absurd
to trust that the baby in young Mary's belly
came from Above; it sounded so silly.
I know what I'd say if I were old Joe.
I'd say something like this, or at least I think so:
"Why can't the Lord choose some other couple?
One already married? For this looks like trouble
to say that a Child will be born unto us.
Why, think of the hassles! Think of the fuss!
And every morning when I shall arise,
I will wake up and look at this Child whose eyes
look nothing like mine. For I cannot boast

of a Child whose Father is the Holy Ghost.
It sounds so preposterous. It is totally wild."
But Joseph just stood there, accepting the Child.
    Joseph just stood there.

When Joseph awoke, he had moved beyond shame.
The baby was born, and he gave it a Name.
"You shall be Jesus," he said with a shout,
"You'll save us from sins, both within and without."
Yet never so much as a word he did speak
about the strange news that the angel did break.
I think that the carpenter was a man's man;
most men don't show feelings if they possibly can.
They step back, removed, and they do not complain.
They observe from a distance; that's part of their pain.
So Joe stood in shadows, remaining obscure.
We don't know much more, though his name does endure.
We assume he provided for them as he could,
with hammers and saws, his hands worked with wood.
We know he dreamed dreams, and the Child protected.
Yet he stayed invisible; no presence detected.
    Joseph just stood there.

Perhaps he was distant, detached, and removed.
A primitive man, and insensitive too.
But if we go deeper, I think we might see
that Joseph can teach us the way we can be.
It's hard just to stand there, especially this season.
There's so much to do, regardless of reason.
We have presents to wrap and bright lights to put up.
Big checks to write out and fat banquets to sup.
It's especially hard if you're a man just like me.
There are places to go and people to see.
Keep busy, keep moving, and don't dare to stop.
Keep working all day, until night when you drop.
So much of men's lives are so breathless in pace.
We sprint all day long, like we're running a race.

It's hard to acknowledge when we're not in charge.
(I like to run things, and have folks call me "Sarge"!)
But the fact of the matter, if honest and true,
is that God gives us Christmas, with nothing to do.
Christ comes as a gift, in deep silence this night.
No action is needed. No stars we must light.
We simply must stand here with arms opened wide,
and give Jesus room to come deep, down, inside.
That, I should mention, is why each December
I need this old story, to help me remember:

 Joseph just stood there.

For all who believe they can manage their clocks,
for all who believe they should work 'til they drop,
for all those who fret, both outside and in pews,
I stand here to say that God gives us good news:
Life doesn't depend on ability to cope,
but upon our good God, in whom we can hope.
The Lord has sent Jesus to set us all free,
to announce God's good favor, and help us to see
we cannot be saved by the work that we do —
we're saved by God's grace, through our faith. This is true!
It's hard to just stand there, to trust and believe.
Especially for those folks who cannot receive.
Yet Joseph can teach us to stand and be still.
Let God give the gift, and with love our hearts fill.
Yes, Christmas means giving, I know that's the drift.
But it's more than mere giving. It's receiving the gift.
So don't just do something, but stand there and sing.
Our Savior is born. Come, worship the King!

 O come, let us adore him!

WHERE CHRISTMAS BEGINS: AMONG THE SHEPHERDS
Luke 2:8-20

8 In that region there were shepherds living in the fields, keeping watch over their flock by night. 9 Then an angel of the Lord stood before them, and the glory of the Lord shone around them, and they were terrified. 10 But the angel said to them, "Do not be afraid; for see — I am bringing you good news of great joy for all the people: 11 to you is born this day in the city of David a Savior, who is the Messiah, the Lord. 12 This will be a sign for you: you will find a child wrapped in bands of cloth and lying in a manger." 13 And suddenly there was with the angel a multitude of the heavenly host, praising God and saying, 14 "Glory to God in the highest heaven, and on earth peace among those whom he favors!"

15 When the angels had left them and gone into heaven, the shepherds said to one another, "Let us go now to Bethlehem and see this thing that has taken place, which the Lord has made known to us." 16 So they went with haste and found Mary and Joseph, and the child lying in the manger. 17 When they saw this, they made known what had been told them about this child; 18 and all who heard it were amazed at what the shepherds told them. 19 But Mary treasured all these words and pondered them in her heart. 20 The shepherds returned, glorifying and praising God for all they had heard and seen, as it had been told them.

Every year we prepare for Christmas at our house by popping a video of *A Charlie Brown Christmas* into the VCR. It's a good story, with great music and wonderful dancing. The line of one character always provokes a chuckle. It's Shermie. Remember him? Lucy is handing out costumes for the Christmas pageant. She goes to Pigpen and Frieda and casts them as the innkeeper and the innkeeper's wife. Then she goes up to a little boy and says, "Shermie, you're a shepherd."

35

Shermie says, "Every year it's the same thing. I always have to be a shepherd."

Admittedly it is not a glamorous part. The shepherds are the anonymous people who suddenly appear at the manger and mill around in adoration. We have no idea how many there were. That may be why, if extra children appear for the Christmas pageant rehearsal, somebody casts them as shepherds. A casting director always has room for more shepherds. Given their traditional pageant headpieces, they could be male or female. Anybody will do.

According to a quick survey, the Wise Men tend to turn up on more Christmas cards. They have the better costumes, after all, and their gold adds a touch of class to the holiday greetings. But the shepherds appear in more Christmas carols. There is something about their humility and simplicity that appeals to our devotion. In fact, the first Christmas carol to be approved for official use by the Church of England was a carol based on Luke's account of the shepherds[1]:

> While shepherds watched their flocks by night,
> All seated on the ground,
> The angel of the Lord came down,
> And glory shone around.

The Christmas story says shepherds came to the birthplace of Jesus. That is a peaceful, idyllic image for most of us. In some ways it may be similar to how urban people subscribe to magazines on country living; they hope to participate in rural life without having to carve their own furniture or build their own compost heaps.

Most of us cannot imagine the hard life of ancient shepherds: traveling as their flocks led them, rarely setting up their tents in the same location twice, devoid of any settled life apart from the rules of clan and nature. Shepherds were people of the land. Their fingernails were always dirty and their skin looked like cracked shoe leather. Chances are, they didn't smell much better than their flocks. Who among us lives like that?

The only shepherds I've ever seen face to face were the ones that posed for photographs in the ancient city of Jericho. The tour buses rolled up, people in baseball caps disembarked, and the shepherds stood stern and noble while cameras clicked and flashed. Somehow those makeshift models did not seem very authentic, even if few tourists passed up the photo opportunity.

On the highway back to Jerusalem from the Dead Sea, we could see tent settlements of modern day Bedouin herders. These days they still maintain an itinerant lifestyle, although they drive Isuzu pickup trucks and use cell phones to manage their flocks. In keeping with ancient tradition, they still avoid city life. The only time they migrate toward town is when it is time to sell either the sheep or their byproducts.

Seeing these shepherds reminds me of all the people who mostly work out of our sight: toll booth operators, emergency room attendants, truck drivers, and studio musicians. Many of them go to work after we have gone to sleep. We depend on them even though we rarely encounter them face-to-face.

Shepherds are not central characters in scripture although they do appear from time to time. King David began his career as a shepherd boy, probably the first rags to riches tale in religious history. When he was questioned about his capability of combating Goliath, he said, "Give me a slingshot, and I can scare off lions, bears, Philistines, and other wild animals" (1 Samuel 17:34-37). His confidence was probably boosted by the knowledge that he had already been secretly anointed as king of Israel (1 Samuel 16:1-13).

Tradition says King David wrote a song wherein he described the God of Israel in terms of his former occupation. "The Lord is my shepherd," he announced, "and under God's care, I have everything I need" (Psalm 23:1). In time, the faithful of Israel added some other verses, most notably the lines from Psalm 100, "Know that the Lord is God. It is he that made us, and we are his; we are his people, and the sheep of his pasture" (Psalm 100:3).

Centuries later, the prophet Ezekiel dreamed of Israel's return from exile. He declared, "Thus says the Lord: I will save my flock, and they shall no longer be ravaged ... and I will set up over them one shepherd, my servant David, and he shall feed them: he shall feed them and be their shepherd" (Ezekiel 34:22-23).

Many years passed, and along with them passed many counterfeit leaders who did not care much about God's flock. Then a young man stood up one day and said, "I am the Good Shepherd. I know my own, and my own know me, just as the Father knows me and I know the Father. And I lay down my life for the sheep" (John 10:14-15).

One time Jesus used a shepherd as a character in a story. "Just imagine," he said, "if you were a shepherd with a hundred sheep in your flock. If one of those sheep got lost, wouldn't you leave the safety of numbers to seek out that lost sheep in the dangerous wilderness?" (Luke 15:4). There is no telling how that story was received, given the risky nature of such a venture.

But it *is* clear that the Gospel writers believed "shepherd" was a good image for Jesus' leadership. Jesus desired to lead people to green pastures and restore their souls. As Jesus was traveling to a deserted place one day, he looked and saw a great crowd of people. "He had compassion on them," says one of the writers, "because they were like sheep without a shepherd; and he began to teach them many things" (Mark 6:34).

Jesus also knew he was the central figure at the heart of their fellowship. Near the end of his life, he warned his closest followers that they would abandon him after his arrest. "For it is written, 'I will strike the shepherd, and the sheep will be scattered'" (Mark 14:26). It was only after the resurrection that the Risen Lord would affirm, "My sheep hear my voice; I know them, and they follow me. I give them eternal life, and no one will snatch them out of my hand" (John 10:27-28).

Given this illustrious background, it may be difficult for us to realize how shepherds developed an unsavory reputation in the first century. Joachim Jeremias, the German scholar, notes that first-century shepherds were refused entrance to the Jerusalem Temple.[2] The religious establishment maintained lists of "despised trades" and shepherds appeared on those lists. They were widely scorned for their dishonesty and considered thieves. As someone once said, "In the time of Jesus, the shepherds were the heroes of all the stories, but you wouldn't want your daughter to marry one."

Two reasons lie behind the stigma against shepherds. First, they led their herds onto land that belonged to other people. The grazing of sheep on the personal property of others was considered a form of stealing. Their habits remind me of the stories my grandfather told about the gypsies who wandered through western Pennsylvania. "You never knew if they would simply show up and camp on your land," he said. "And when they did, you couldn't get rid of them. They acted as if they owned the place."

The second, and deeper, reason why religious people in the first century shunned the shepherds had to do with the indiscriminate diet of the sheep. They would graze literally *anywhere*. Since every herder was responsible for the actions of the animals, shepherds could never know how many people had been wronged. Shepherds could never make amends for those whom they had injured or cheated. Therefore, *the people they had wronged could never have forgiven them.*

So what is Luke saying when he announces that God sent an angel — *not* to the temple, *not* to the religious list-keepers — *but to the shepherds*?

According to Luke, this is the good news of God in its clearest expression. God's kingdom is given to those who do not deserve it, to those who could never earn their way. The great banquet of heaven is offered as a gift to the poor, the crippled, the lame, and the blind (14:13). Grace is dished out to the sinner and the misfit (19:1-10). Blessings are pronounced upon the poor, the hungry, and those who are hated (6:20-22). Prodigals are welcomed back to the father's table, even before they can complete their well-rehearsed repentance speeches (15:20-22). God reconciles sinners even before they can stand comfortably in God's presence (18:13-14). And for the time being on Christmas Eve, these wandering shepherds are invited home.

One year at a Sunday school production of the Christmas story, some young children dressed as shepherds were seated off to the side of the church's chancel. In the center of the makeshift stage, the angel appeared to announce Jesus' birth, first to Mary, and then to Joseph. The children dressed as shepherds couldn't hear very well. Since all the action was going on elsewhere, they began to whisper, and then talk among themselves.

Some of them weren't paying attention when the angel came over to speak to them. It caught them by surprise. Then the host of angels suddenly appeared to say, "Glory to God in the highest heaven, and on earth peace among those whom God favors."

This caught the attention of the smallest shepherd, one of the ones who had been wiggling the most. He tugged on his big sister's bathrobe and said in a hoarse voice, "What did they say?"

She turned and said with an authoritative voice, "They said God likes you!"

To which the littlest shepherd replied, "He does?"

That's where Christmas begins. As if to underscore God's generosity, Luke tells how the shepherds received the good news of Jesus' birth while the leaders of the known world are left in the dark. Remember how the story begins?

> *In those days a decree went out from Emperor Augustus that all the world should be registered. This was the first registration and was taken while Quirinius was governor of Syria ...*

We should not miss the irony of this introduction. As a pompous Emperor across the sea demands his officials to write down every name and count every person, an angel is dispatched from God to a group of *anonymous* shepherds. To this day nobody but God knows their names. According to the bureaucrats in distant Rome, those shepherds are people who will never "count." Yet to God they matter as much as anybody else — maybe even a little bit more so.

And so Christmas begins ... among the shepherds. As the old Christmas carol continues:

> *To you in David's town this day*
> *Is born of David's line*
> *A Savior, who is Christ the Lord;*
> *And this shall be the sign:*

40

The heavenly Babe you there shall find
To human view displayed,
All meanly wrapped in swathing bands,
And in a manger laid.

A few years ago, religion columnist Gustav Niebuhr wrote a front-page article for *The New York Times*. It was the December 24 edition and he asked, "What about the people who wander into church tonight?" Here's the issue, he said:

> *On Christmas Eve, the view from the pulpit is not what a preacher sees on a typical Sunday morning. The holiday congregation includes not only the regular reverent, but also no shortage of the sleepy, the fidgety, and the festive people whose evenings probably began with a party.*
>
> *At churches across the country, "Christmas Christians" pose a seasonal challenge, one with both a mundane and a spiritual dimension. As members of the clergy prepare their Christmas Eve sermons and services, they must wrestle with how to treat the year-end swelling of their flock. Do they simply welcome them, and try to squeeze them into a suddenly overcrowded church, or do they temper their greetings with a note of reproof? Even more importantly, how can they touch their souls so deeply that they will entice them to come back soon?[3]*

As Niebuhr asked these questions, he heard all kinds of answers. A softhearted priest in Oklahoma suggested that Christmas Eve is not the time to scold outsiders. A Presbyterian preacher in New York City admitted he gives a humorous jab to his visitors, saying, "By the way, we do this every Sunday at 11:00." In one church, it was reported a parishioner once took a swing at an usher after the usher said there were no more seats in the sanctuary. One enterprising pastor even decided to turn the event into a fund-raiser, and auctioned off a prime parking space and pew for a Christmas Eve service. One year it went for $500.

41

The best reply, however, came from a Lutheran minister in Circle Pines, Minnesota. "It's not my sole responsibility if any of them ever come back," she said. "My little sermon will only amount to a single sentence in God's lifelong conversation with each person."

"I'm just glad they're in church," she said, "because I have one more chance to tell them the story, one more chance to say, 'God is with you.' "

Do you remember what the angel said to those shepherds? "To you is born this day in the city of David a Savior, who is the Messiah, the Lord." To you, of all people. Not only to the history makers, not merely to those who are habitually religious, but to you. All of you.

What should we do if shepherds show up on Christmas Eve? Give them a candle. Invite them to sing.

1. *The Penguin Book of Carols*, Ian Bradley, editor (New York: Penguin Putnam, 1999), p. 395.

2. Joachim Jeremias, *Jerusalem in the Time of Jesus: An Investigation into Economic and Social Conditions During the New Testament Period* (Minneapolis: Fortress Press, 1962), pp. 303-312.

3. Gustav Niebuhr, "Predicament in the Pulpit: The Christmas Eve Crowd," *The New York Times*, December 24, 1996.

FOR THE SHEPHERDS
Luke 2:1-20

"The first Nowell the angel did say
was to certain poor shepherds in fields as they lay."
It's a strange twist of Christmas to put it that way,
to say God's good news was announced on that day
to *shepherds*, not kings. Yet this night we say,
　　"Christmas comes for shepherds."

As we hear the old story we never do learn
the names of those shepherds whose news we return.
Other characters we've met, in books here and there.
We know who they were, when they lived, how and where.
Augustus, we know, was the world's greatest leader,
And Governor Quirinius, Rome's puppet in Syria.
We know Joseph Carpenter and young mother Mary,
and the angel called Gabriel whose presence was scary.
Don't forget Zechariah and his wife, old Aunt Liz,
and the son they named John (in the baptism biz).
The crafty, cruel king in the big showy palace
was named Herod of Judea in spite of his malice.
But the shepherds had no names, at least none that we know.
They were nobodies from nowhere asleep in the snow.
Anonymous folk who lived in a field,
They moved with their flocks as the grazing would yield.
We don't know their names. They weren't Bruce, Bob, or Ed.
No names and no stories, just faces instead.
But to them came the news from glory on high
that in King David's birthplace a Savior was nigh.
　　Christmas comes for shepherds.

We might prefer kings, for they have the power
to shake up the world in less than an hour.
From the thrones of the world, a simple command
can send soldiers to war or claim someone's land.
A king can move mountains with a minor decree,

send rebels away across land or the sea.
What a thrill it would be to convert all the kings!
To compel them to peace. To teach them to sing.
But it's clear from the story that all those in power
were pawns in God's plan to birth Christ at that hour.
Augustus, for instance, announced the first census
to keep track of his tax base, his lands, and his fences.
But he didn't know that God, in his glory,
worked in the dark shadows to fulfill an old story.
For Joseph and Mary went to Bethlehem town,
where David was born, grew up, got his crown.
They paid up their taxes, as hoped that they would,
and bunked with some family in the old neighborhood.
Then around midnight, Mary's water did break.
That young mother was frightened and started to shake.
Before she even knew it, baby Jesus was born.
With no cradle nearby and the cows in the corn
she put him in a feed trough and cooed him to sleep.
Through his first fragile night, the angels did keep.
Augustus never learned that a new king was born,
for Christmas didn't come to him on that morn.

  Christmas comes for shepherds.

"Why shepherds?" you ask. I admit I don't know.
They were coarse. They were crude, the lowest of low.
The rabbis kept lists of the good folks and bad.
Some made them happy, and some made them mad.
The rabbis thought shepherds were nothing but trouble.
"If you see one around, throw him out on the double!"
They saw shepherds as thieves with little regard
for the personal property of a neighbor's green yard.
The sheep would start grazing. On grass they would munch.
A neighbor's new landscaping became a sheep's lunch.
"That's stealing!" said neighbors. The rabbis agreed.
They warned the sheep herders, who in turn would not heed.
"What's more," said the rabbis, reflecting a bit,
"when we gather for worship, the shepherds will skip.

44

They claim to work weekends. We know it is true,
yet come a free Sabbath, other things they will do."
In a way you can't blame them, as herders of sheep,
for sheep will eat anything. God's Law they don't keep.
And sometimes the food that a sheep will digest
is dirty at worst and unclean at best.
A shepherd is liable for what his sheep will eat.
If they eat something sinful, the owner can't beat
the long list of sins that his sheep have committed.
They both break God's law and nothing's omitted.
So why should a shepherd go off to the temple?
There's no easy forgiveness. The sins aren't that simple.
    But Christmas comes for shepherds.

For here is the wonder of Christmas that night.
No matter the darkness, God offers some light.
No matter the distance, God bridges the gap.
So Gabriel woke them right up from their nap.
The angel was holy, a messenger great.
"Listen," he said, "and I'll set you straight.
A Savior is born in David's hometown.
He forgives all our sins. He lightens each frown.
And the best news of all may sound even stranger.
The Savior's a babe who lies in a manger.
Look for this child dressed up in blue.
There you'll find mercy for me and for you."
    Christmas comes for shepherds.

Now ponder this message from their point of view.
And note how they handled this word that was new.
For shepherds are wanderers, people who roam
from place unto place, with no permanent home.
Like modern-day truckers hitting the road,
they migrated daily and carried their load.
They never stayed planted in one place too long.
They kept on the go and did nowhere belong.
Let's face it: the shepherds were traveling folk.

But something did change when Gabriel spoke.
The shepherds left flocks and went right away
to see this new wonder that God had just made.
They left all their tents and went to the town,
to catch just a glimpse of a world upside-down.
And what to their curious eyes did appear?
But God in a manger, in a Child so dear.
They thought God lived high in the sky far away.
Yet now God-is-with-us to live and to stay.
That Presence burns hot with the judgment of grace,
and allows us to see the kind smile on God's Face.
This is, in all essence, what angels did say
to certain poor shepherds in fields as they lay:
God knows you. God loves you. God gives you a home.
God shepherds the shepherds wherever they roam.
     Christmas comes for shepherds.

Shepherds still wander to a place such as this,
reeking of angels, in search of God's kiss.
Maybe they think they can camp on the lawn
or come near the temple and stifle a yawn.
Whatever the case, don't despise the poor shepherds.
They travel as pilgrims in search of good words,
and sit in our midst because angels have sung.
They want to know truly if God's love has done
this marvelous thing that we're singing about:
of a Babe born this day with a prayer and a shout.
So welcome the shepherds and give them a space,
for God has been working in their time and place.
That, after all, is why Christmas has come,
to give the nameless a Name and the homeless a Home.
Don't despise the poor shepherds for God does them bring.
But give them a candle. Invite them to sing.
     Christmas comes for shepherds.

WHERE CHRISTMAS REACHES:
TO THE ENDS OF THE EARTH
Matthew 2:1-12

> *1 In the time of King Herod, after Jesus was born in Bethlehem of Judea, wise men from the East came to Jerusalem, 2 asking, "Where is the child who has been born king of the Jews? For we observed his star at its rising, and have come to pay him homage." 3 When King Herod heard this, he was frightened, and all Jerusalem with him; 4 and calling together all the chief priests and scribes of the people, he inquired of them where the Messiah was to be born. 5 They told him, "In Bethlehem of Judea; for so it has been written by the prophet: 6 'And you, Bethlehem, in the land of Judah, are by no means least among the rulers of Judah; for from you shall come a ruler who is to shepherd my people Israel.'"*

> *7 Then Herod secretly called for the wise men and learned from them the exact time when the star had appeared. 8 Then he sent them to Bethlehem, saying, "Go and search diligently for the child; and when you have found him, bring me word so that I may also go and pay him homage." 9 When they had heard the king, they set out; and there, ahead of them, went the star that they had seen at its rising, until it stopped over the place where the child was. 10 When they saw that the star had stopped, they were overwhelmed with joy. 11 On entering the house, they saw the child with Mary his mother; and they knelt down and paid him homage. Then, opening their treasure chests, they offered him gifts of gold, frankincense, and myrrh. 12 And having been warned in a dream not to return to Herod, they left for their own country by another road.*

It is striking how many Christmas cards portray the three Wise Men. They are favored figures in our holiday greetings, usually depicted in jeweled turbans and luxurious robes as they ride their camels across the moonlit horizon. Their presence gives an outlandish touch to the familiar Christmas story. Arriving late, they present extravagant gifts to the newborn child. Leaving early, they disappear from the pages of scripture and are never heard from again.

Like Luke, Matthew tells of strange visitors to the infant Jesus. The Wise Men from the East are the most exotic members of our crèche scene. Their presence is totally unexpected, for they are the last people anybody would think to see at the child's home. Yet they come bidden by a phenomenon in the night sky, somehow discerning that a new Jewish king has been born.

The Bible does not actually tell us how many Wise Men arrived or the size of their entourage. Ever since 1857, when John Henry Hopkins, Jr., composed "We Three Kings Of Orient Are," the number three has been fixed in our consciousness. There were three gifts of gold, frankincense, and myrrh, so the assumption is each gift was carried by a different visitor. While there is no reason to doubt this commonly held belief, it should be noted that ancient sources outside the Bible also numbered them as two, four, or twelve.

Their names are equally unknown. The favorite tradition names them as Balthasar, with dark skin and a beard; Melchior, an aged man with white skin and a beard; and Gaspar, a young white man with pink cheeks. The diversity of these descriptions is striking. It points to the wider inclusion of those in future generations that will worship and follow Jesus. Raymond Brown believes that, in telling this story, Matthew was anticipating the Gentile Christians of his own time and place.[1] Maybe so. To this day, we see our own faces in these ancient travelers whose wisdom is revealed in their worship.

But who, or what, were the magi? The historian Herodotus wrote of a caste of priests called magi who lived in ancient Persia. They practiced the dualistic religion of Zoroastrianism, and their specialty was interpreting dreams. Philo of Alexandria complimented the magi of his day for their knowledge and understanding of nature. In the New Testament, two other magi are named: Simon

Magus (Acts 8:9-24) and Elymas (Acts 13:6-11). According to the Acts of the Apostles, these were unsavory characters who misunderstood the gospel and undermined its proclamation.

As Raymond Brown summarizes his research, "The term 'magi' refers to those engaged in occult arts and covers a wide range of astrologers, fortune tellers, priestly augurers, and magicians of various plausibility."[2] If so, these were people who would be regarded in traditional Jewish piety as heretics and outsiders. The Torah forbids contact with such people.[3] Christians, like their older Jewish siblings, believe in the One God of Moses. We do not need to seek guidance from any extraneous sources. Nor do we find it necessary to check our horoscopes before leaving home each morning. God's guidance is sufficient.

Yet here they are: the ancient equivalent of three staff members from the Psychic Friends Network paying a call on the newborn Prince of Peace. Their presence is jarring, to say the least. And their quest is unexpected: "Where is the child who has been born king of the Jews? For we observed his star at its rising, and have come to pay him homage." Their attention to the natural world has caused them to search for Jesus. They seek him, but they do not know where to find him.

Herod himself has no clue where the Christ child can be found. He is the incumbent king, after all. Herod has not spent much time thinking about his successor. At first the king is frightened by the news, fearful that he will be dethroned. It isn't long, however, before Herod becomes curious. He calls in a group of religious professionals and says, "Tell me where the Messiah is to be born." They answer him with the words from the prophet Micah:

And you, Bethlehem, in the land of Judah,
are by no means least among the rulers of Judah;
for from you shall come a ruler
who is to shepherd my people Israel. — Micah 5:2

As the following poem suggests, true faith brings together an awareness of the world with the knowledge of the scriptures. The

49

magi seek the newborn king, yet have many unanswered questions.[4] Where is he born? To what royal family? Under what political circumstances? What kind of king will he be? The magi cannot presume to know. Their knowledge is incomplete. As Garrison Keillor once quipped, "If you get your guidance by following a star, the directions are going to be a little bit vague."[5]

At the same time, the very people among whom the Messiah is born — the people of Jerusalem, the chief priests, and the scribes — have not been paying attention to God's work in and above the world. They may have hoped and prayed for a deliverer, but they were not actively expecting him. Like Herod, they might have known his name — Messiah — but they were unwilling to be unseated by his grace. As one scholar writes:

> *One can, like the chief priests and scribes, know the biblical facts but completely miss the deeper biblical truth. One can memorize verses, but forget the gospel. One can recite the kings of Israel and overlook the King of Creation. One can, like Herod, be in favor of studying the scripture and still be on the wrong side of God's will.*[6]

The contrast between the characters of this story is striking. The Wise Men ponder the mysteries in the sky. They discern God is up to something, yet remain uncertain where it might be happening. They need the scriptures to clarify and confirm their search. The chief priests and scribes have the ancient scrolls at their disposal, but they are removed from the experience of awe that the Wise Men can claim. As Matthew's book unfolds, it also becomes painfully clear that they refuse to worship the Messiah as the magi intend to do. Meanwhile King Herod, who cares little about the star or the scriptures, misuses the information he receives and initiates a massacre.

The Wise Men, in their own way, share the awe of the shepherds in Luke's story. They have not been beckoned by an angelic voice. In no way do they represent the dispossessed or the poor of Israel. They are Gentiles, outsiders in every way. Yet they are strangely attracted to the Christ child, and they travel at great cost to find him. This is God's doing. The magi's search begins with a star that only God could have put into the sky. During the journey, the inference is that they are protected by divine providence. Even after they find the One for whom they were looking, God warns them in a dream to avoid Herod and go home by another road.

Even though they were outsiders to the promises and stories of Israel, God found a way to include them. Without dropping his usual footnote ("this was to fulfill ..."), Matthew is reminding us of a prophetic text from Isaiah 60:1-6.

> *Arise, shine; for your light has come,*
> *and the glory of the Lord has risen upon you.*
> *For darkness shall cover the earth,*
> *and thick darkness the peoples;*
> *but the Lord will arise upon you,*
> *and his glory will appear over you.*
> *Nations shall come to your light,*
> *and kings to the brightness of your dawn.*
> *Lift up your eyes and look around;*
> *they all gather together, they come to you;*
> *your sons shall come from far away,*
> *and your daughters shall be carried*
> *on their nurses' arms.*
> *Then you shall see and be radiant;*
> *your heart shall thrill and rejoice,*
> *because the abundance of the sea*
> *shall be brought to you,*
> *the wealth of the nations shall come to you.*
> *A multitude of camels shall cover you,*
> *the young camels of Midian and Ephah;*
> *all those from Sheba shall come.*
> *They shall bring* gold *and* frankincense,
> *and shall proclaim the praise of the Lord.*

The prophet Isaiah announced, "Nations shall come to your light." The Hebrew term for "nations" is *goyim*, often translated as "the Gentiles" and exemplified in these exotic visitors from the East. The glory of the Lord, depicted metaphorically as a Light, attracts people of other races beyond Israel. In the vision of Isaiah, worshipers of God come from Midian, Ephah, Sheba, Kedar, and Mebaioth. The vision finds fulfillment in the unexpected arrival of the magi, who will later be elevated by theological tradition and become three "kings."

As Matthew tells the story of Jesus' birth, he reminds us of the international appeal of the newborn savior. The infant Jesus is the Messiah, the fulfillment of God's promises to Israel. He is also the Light that draws people from all the nations of the world. No restriction is placed on those who will be drawn to him. The light of Christ will shine to the ends of the earth.

Matthew scores an additional theological point by announcing the gifts of the magi. Like the anticipated outsiders of Isaiah's prophecy, the Wise Men bring gold and frankincense, two appropriate gifts for a sovereign. They also bring myrrh, an ancient *burial spice*. How strange! It is analogous to delivering a gallon of embalming fluid to the maternity ward, or signing up a newborn infant for a cemetery plot.

Why bring myrrh? Jesus is still an infant and already the magi are honoring his death. Matthew is introducing Jesus as a child who is born in order to die. The Messiah will teach and heal, to be sure. Yet his greatest significance will be seen in the events surrounding, and following, his death. King Herod will not succeed in snuffing out Jesus' life. The chief priests and scribes of Herod's court will be replaced some thirty years later by others who will oversee Jesus' crucifixion. But no one will thwart the purposes of God. In his death and resurrection, Jesus will draw all kinds of people to himself.

Matthew makes this clear in the closing story of his Gospel. The Risen Christ stands with his disciples on a mountain in Galilee. Before he commissions them to make disciples of all nations, Matthew says, "They worshiped him." That is, by the end of the story, Jesus' followers paid him homage, just like the magi did at the beginning.[7]

This is the end toward which the whole Christmas story directs us: to worship Christ, the newborn king. As the ancient sages are invited to "leave their contemplations," so we are invited to bend our knees and speak the truth with our tongues. Jesus Christ is the sovereign lord of God's creation, king over all other kings, crowned by the praises of those who love him.

1. Raymond Brown, *The Birth of the Messiah* (New York: Doubleday, 1977), pp. 199-200.

2. Brown, 167.

3. See Leviticus 20:6, 20:26, and Deuteronomy 18:10-14.

4. Some of the following material is drawn from my sermon, "What a Star Can't Tell You," published in *Praying For A Whole New World* (Lima, Ohio: CSS Publishing, 2000).

5. From one of Keillor's unpublished Lake Wobegon monologues, broadcast on National Public Radio. Mr. Keillor is particularly fond of the magi, and they appear frequently in his Christmas stories.

6. Thomas G. Long, *Matthew* (Louisville: Westminster John Knox, 1997), p. 19.

7. The Greek verb for "worship" and "pay homage" is *proskuneo*. It is a word with calisthenic overtones, referring to bending one's knee or prostrating oneself as an act of awe and worship. A favorite word for Matthew, it is used thirteen times in the first Gospel, all but twice in reference to how people approach Jesus Christ.

WHERE HAVE THE WISE MEN GONE?
Matthew 2:1-12

A crèche on a table is missing some pieces.
It has Mary and Joseph, and small baby Jesus.
The shepherds are present, and quaking with fear.
They were summoned by angels in fields quite near.
Some cattle and sheep are standing at hand.
A star on the roof shines good news through the land.
But three figures are absent. They are nowhere in sight.
Apparently they disappeared in the night.
A young girl with curls clued in right away.
She pointed it out to her daddy one day.
"Look, Daddy," she whispered, "the Wise Men aren't here.
Were they still in a box? Or did they disappear?"
He had no idea where they might be found.
Three figures had vanished. They were not around.
　　　Where have the Wise Men gone?

In Matthew, they're "magi" and not three wee kings.
It's misleading to hear the old carol we sing.
Probably not kings, but wise men and sages
who studied the heavens throughout all the ages.
No one can number the magi for sure,
but the number three certainly does endure.
If they brought three gifts, so the reasoning goes,
there must be three Wise Men (as everyone knows).
Tradition has given a name to each one,
although true identities will never be known.
Old bearded Melchior carried gold for a king.
Blushing young Gaspar, his incense did bring.
A man with dark skin was named Balthasar.
Myrrh was the spice that he brought from afar.
And of these three gifts, myrrh should raise up our eyes.
It's an embalming spice for a Child born to die.
We can't say for certain if this was the buzz,
but we do know the Wise Men looked something like us.

For they were the *goyim*, the Gentiles outside
the promises of Israel. And they did abide
in places like Persia (that is, Babylon),
the site of the Exile where Israel had gone.
As ancient astrologers, they read signs in the sky
and studied the stars, marking wonders up high.
These days, our magi will read horoscopes
to look for some guidance and bolster their hopes.
In search of direction, what to do, what to be,
they will turn to the psychics on cable TV.
The point is: they didn't know scripture, God's story.
The magi knew mystery, but knew not God's glory.
They read nature's face and sensed holiness was lurking,
yet they did not know what surprise God was working.
They discerned a new king was about to be born,
but they didn't know where, how, or when — on what morn.
With something like faith that seeks understanding,
they climbed on their camels, all three of them banding
to journey some distance to countries afar,
quite simply because they had seen a new star.
Now, most of us wish for more tangible proof.
We don't want to wander and learn it's a goof.
So give them some credit, though they knew not God's game.
Attuned to deep mystery, they came seeking the Name.
How strange such outsiders were gathered by grace:
Exotic and Gentile, yet in God's embrace.
        Yet where have the Wise Men gone?

One answer, I think, comes with some sobriety,
and slices through popular notions of piety.
The crèche comes from Luke, at least technically speaking.
Luke alone thinks the scene bears some repeating.
Mary wrapped Jesus to lie in a manger.
According to Luke, he was not in danger.
Joseph just stood there, and Mary did ponder,
while a few peasants' animals around them did wander.

Then shepherds arrived, in their odd adoration,
as angels sang songs of annunciation.
The crèche seems so gentle, an idyllic scene.
We almost forget that the world is so mean.
Matthew says otherwise, and gives candid news
of evil, deception, and power's abuse.
In Matt's Christmas story, God gives constant warning
to those near the Child. His birth on that morning
did announce death of deadliness in this age;
yet Herod, we know, still erupts in a rage.
Listen: this world gives out crosses to carry.
Those righteous and innocent, this age wants to bury.
After seeing the Child, the wise men dreamed fear.
When God warned, "Get moving," they didn't stay near.
So we shouldn't expect to see them in a crèche.
They didn't stay long enough to risk their necks.
Their absence, I guess, is a sign for the brave
of this present world that the Christ came to save.
Where life is at risk, the question not needed
is, "Where are the Wise Men?" for God's warning they heeded.
        Yet where have the Wise Men gone?

I ask, since devotion is the gift which they bring
in traveling far distance in search of a King.
They stand in sharp contrast to those in the palace,
who lived in dark shadows of evil and malice.
The magi went first to search there for the king;
a logical place for true homage to bring.
Yet when they arrived, it was worse than suspected.
The king whom they met wasn't whom they expected.
That king's name was Herod, and he was quite sly.
When he spoke of "worship," it was a great lie.
For kings cannot worship while sitting on thrones.
They're distracted by greatness that seeps through their bones.
This Herod had priests on his payroll, it seems,
to manage his critics and justify his schemes.

When Wise Men came ignorant of the Christ's birth,
Herod beckoned to priests and asked them with mirth,
"Would you look to the scriptures and fill in our gaps?
Then go back to your rooms and back to your naps.
We'd like to ... worship ... the new baby King."
But he didn't mean it, for he didn't sing.
Herod couldn't adore him. Not that kind of man,
who co-opted priests to short-circuit God's plan.
He turned to the scriptures to justify himself,
then he put them back up on that high, dusty shelf.
What's lacking? Devotion. And wisdom so true
that begins with the fear of a God who can do
some holy, fierce wonders on which we depend.
Our God dethrones all whose knees will not bend.
We learn our example in those from the East.
They did not know scripture, but their lives were a feast
of gratitude and praise that were given in freedom.
These are two true signs of God's present kingdom.
Devotion and scripture, when they go hand in hand,
will unveil Christ who draws near to our land.
Remembering this, let's return to the issue
before someone wraps me in ribbon and tissue;
     namely, where have the Wise Men gone?

"They went home by another way" — that's where they went.
Tired and weary, most likely well spent.
No longer at ease "in the old dispensation,"
a new King was enthroned upon their adoration.
For long before Jesus grew up among Jews,
the Wise Men were home, out spreading the news.
Those unlikely Persians who read horoscopes
now pointed to Israel as the source of their hopes.
And like a small seed that is planted by hand,
God's Kingdom took root throughout foreign land.
"Where have the Wise Men gone?" might we ask.
They have gone home, to begin a new task.
Look: most here are Gentiles, like Wise Men of old.

We depend on their message, just as we've been told.
The witness of magi should be said loud and clear.
If it weren't for the Wise Men, we wouldn't be here.

Some still worship stars, or do hocus-pocus,
or live by vague hungers that lack a clear focus.
Others live in big palaces and over-consume.
They grow weary of grace, and that is their doom.
And consider this world where we live and we die:
Innocents still slaughtered; our leaders still lie.
Yet God is here, too, in some ways quite concealed.
Our work is announcing the Good News revealed
to Wise Men and Wise Women whose hearts are awake.
We tell them how Christ has been born for our sake.
For here is our King, who lies sweet in the manger.
He was born in a world that is filled up with danger.
The Christ is the King above all other kings,
and those bruised by this world are the first ones to sing.
Their song now continues to swell through the air,
until every last person is free from despair.
We join in that song which will win over fear,
for magi have told us that God has come near.
And our God will triumph. We'll see in the end,
when each tongue confesses and each knee shall bend.
    Come and worship! Come and worship!
    Worship Christ the newborn King!

SERVICE #1 — MARY, PONDER THIS

SERVICE OF LESSONS AND CAROLS

Prelude

Lighting of the Christ Candle

Call to Worship   Luke 1:52-55
The Lord has brought down the mighty from their thrones,
  The Lord has lifted up the lowly.
The Lord has filled the hungry with good things,
  The Lord has sent the rich away empty.
The Lord has helped his servant Israel,
  according to the promise he made to our ancestors.

Hymn   "O Come, All Ye Faithful"

Prayer of Adoration
  Holy and powerful God,
  you have come to us in the Child of Mary.
  You have taken on our vulnerable flesh,
  and chosen to dwell among human weakness.
  How amazing are your ways!
  Awaken our faith this night,
  that we would believe your Word,
  trust your power,
  and welcome your grace.
  This we pray through Jesus Christ our Lord,
  who lives and reigns with you
  in the unity of the Holy Spirit,
  one God, forever and ever. Amen.

Passing the Peace

Response (to "O Come, All Ye Faithful")
  O come, let us adore him! O come, let us adore him!
  O come, let us adore him, Christ the Lord!

Welcome

Prayer for Illumination

Lesson	Isaiah 7:10-16
Carol	"O Come, O Come, Emmanuel"
Lesson	Micah 5:2-4
Carol	"O Little Town Of Bethlehem"
Lesson	Luke 1:26-38
Carol	"The Angel Gabriel From Heaven Came"
Lesson	Luke 1:39-45
Carol	"Song Of Mary" (or another setting of the Magnificat)
Lesson	Luke 2:1-7
Carol	"Gentle Mary Laid Her Child"
Lesson	Luke 2:8-18, 20
Carol	"Angels We Have Heard On High"
Lesson	Luke 1:34; 2:19, 34
Sermon	"Mary, Ponder This"
Anthem	"Mary, Did You Know?" (by Mark Lowry and Buddy Green, arranged by Fred Bock, published by Fred Bock Music Company item #BG2326)

Affirmation of Faith from John 1:1-14

> In the beginning was the Word, and the Word was with
> God, and the Word was God.
> All things came into being through him,
> and without him not one thing came into being.
> He was in the world, and the world came into being through
> him; yet the world did not know him.
> He came to what was his own,
> and his own people did not accept him.
> But to all who received him, who believed in his name,
> he gave power to become children of God,
> who were born, not of blood or of the will of the flesh
> or of the will of man, but of God.
> And the Word became flesh and lived among us,
> and we have seen his glory,
> the glory as of a father's only son, full of grace and
> truth.

Offering

Offertory

Prayer of Thanksgiving and the Lord's Prayer
The Lord be with you.
> **And also with you.**
Let us give thanks to the Lord our God.
> **It is right to give our thanks and praise.**
Let us pray ...

Hymn   "Silent Night, Holy Night"

Charge and Benediction

Postlude

SERVICE #2 — JOSEPH, JUST STAND THERE

SERVICE OF LESSONS AND CAROLS

Prelude

Lighting of the Christ Candle

Call to Worship   Matthew 1:23
Look, the virgin shall conceive and bear a son,
And they shall name him Emmanuel,
which means "God with us."

Hymn   "Joy To The World"

Prayer of Adoration
O God whose strength is present in silence:
we worship and adore you in the stillness of your Spirit.
In every age you have called your children to live holy lives.
You have led us in paths of righteousness for your name's
   sake.
This night, prepare us for the surprises of your grace,
that we might discern your ways
and follow as you lead us in freedom, righteousness,
   and love;
through Jesus Christ our Lord,
who lives and reigns with you
in the unity of the Holy Spirit,
one God, forever and ever. Amen.

Passing the Peace

Response (to "Joy To The World")
And wonders of His love, and wonders of His love,
And wonders, and wonders, of His love.

Welcome

Prayer for Illumination

Lesson	Isaiah 11:1-9
Carol	"Lo, How A Rose E'er Blooming"
Lesson	Isaiah 40:1-8
Carol	"Comfort, Comfort You My People"
Lesson	Micah 4:1-5
Carol	"Lift Up Your Heads, Ye Mighty Gates"
Lesson	Matthew 1:1, 12-17
Carol	"It Came Upon A Midnight Clear"
Lesson	Matthew 1:18-21
Carol	"Good Christian Friends, Rejoice"
Lesson	Matthew 1:22-25
Sermon	"Joseph, Just Stand There"
Hymn	"Away In A Manger"

Affirmation of Faith Titus 3:4-7
> **When the goodness and kindness of God our Savior appeared, he saved us,**
>> **not because of any works of righteousness that we had done,**
>> **but according to his mercy,**
>> **through the water of rebirth and renewal by the Holy Spirit.**

**This Spirit he poured out on us richly
through Jesus Christ our Savior,
so that, having been justified by his grace,
we might become heirs according to the hope of eternal life.**

Offering

Offertory

Prayer of Thanksgiving and the Lord's Prayer
The Lord be with you.
And also with you.
Let us give thanks to the Lord our God.
It is right to give our thanks and praise.
Let us pray ...

Hymn   "Once In Royal David's City"

Charge and Benediction

Postlude

SERVICE #3 — FOR THE SHEPHERDS

SERVICE OF LESSONS AND CAROLS

Prelude

Lighting of the Christ Candle

Call to Worship   from Luke 2:10-14
Do not be afraid; for I am bringing you good news of a great joy
for all the people.
> **To you is born this day in the city of David a Savior,**
> **who is the Messiah, the Lord.**
Glory to God in the highest heaven,
> **And on earth peace among those whom God favors.**

Hymn   "Angels, From The Realms Of Glory"

Prayer of Adoration
> **O God our savior,**
> **the mystery of your grace**
> **has turned the world upside-down.**
> **Outsiders are included in your promises,**
> **strangers are invited to your table,**
> **and sinners are forgiven.**
> **You welcome us with the hospitality of the gospel,**
> **and we are grateful for your surprising love.**
> **Give us a proper opinion of ourselves,**
> **that we might serve others in your name**
> **and rely on you for all our needs;**
> **through Jesus Christ our Lord,**
> **who lives and reigns with you**
> **in the unity of the Holy Spirit,**
> **one God, forever and ever. Amen.**

Passing the Peace

Prayer for Illumination

Lesson	2 Samuel 7:8-13
Carol	"Come, Thou Long-Expected Jesus"
Lesson	Psalm 23
Carol	"Rise Up, Shepherd, And Follow"
Lesson	Ezekiel 34:11-16
Carol	"See Amid The Winter's Snow"
Lesson	Luke 15:4-7
Carol	"Go Tell It On The Mountain"
Lesson	Luke 2:1-7
Carol	"What Child Is This"
Lesson	Luke 2:8-14
Carol	"While Shepherds Watched Their Flocks"
Lesson	Luke 2:15-20
Sermon	"For The Shepherds"
Hymn	"Angels We Have Heard On High"

Affirmation of Faith Titus 3:4-7
When the goodness and kindness of God our Savior appeared, he saved us,

not because of any works of righteousness that we had done,
but according to his mercy,
through the water of rebirth and renewal by the Holy Spirit.
This Spirit he poured out on us richly
through Jesus Christ our Savior,
so that, having been justified by his grace,
we might become heirs according to the hope of eternal life.

Offering

Offertory

Prayer of Thanksgiving and the Lord's Prayer
The Lord be with you.
And also with you.
Let us give thanks to the Lord our God.
It is right to give our thanks and praise.
Let us pray ...

Hymn   "Infant Holy, Infant Lowly"

Charge and Benediction

Postlude

SERVICE #4 — WHERE HAVE THE WISE MEN GONE?

SERVICE OF LESSONS AND CAROLS

Prelude

Call to Worship   from Isaiah 60
Arise, shine, for your light is come!
    The glory of the Lord is risen upon you!
Nations shall come to your light,
    And rulers to the brightness of your dawn.

Hymn   "Brightest And Best Of The Stars Of The Morning"

Prayer of Adoration
    Almighty God,
    you have sent Jesus Christ to be the light of the world.
    The world has been illumined
    by the power of his presence.
    His truthfulness exposes our sin.
    His mercy reveals your grace.
    Grant that we might serve you in the light of Christ's love,
    and show forth the wisdom of the gospel;
    through Jesus Christ our Lord,
    who lives and reigns with you
    in the unity of the Holy Spirit,
    one God, forever and ever. Amen.

Passing the Peace

Prayer for Illumination

Lesson   Isaiah 9:2-7

Carol   "Break Forth, O Beauteous Heavenly Light"

Lesson   Isaiah 60:1-6

Carol	"What Star Is This, With Beams So Bright?"
Lesson	Micah 5:2-5
Carol	"On This Day Earth Shall Ring"
Lesson	Luke 1:68-79
Carol	"Song Of Zechariah"
Lesson	1 John 1:1-5
Carol	"Hark, The Herald Angels Sing"
Lesson	Matthew 2:1-12
Sermon	"Where Have The Wise Men Gone?"
Carol	"We Three Kings Of Orient Are"

Affirmation of Faith: Nicene Creed

Offering

Offertory	"Coventry Carol"

Prayer of Thanksgiving and the Lord's Prayer
The Lord be with you.
   And also with you.
Let us give thanks to the Lord our God.
   It is right to give our thanks and praise.
Let us pray ...

Hymn	"As With Gladness Men Of Old"

Charge and Benediction

Postlude